The Secret Garden

THE SECRET GARDEN

First presented at the Polka Theatre, Wimbledon, London
on 13th February 1997 with the following cast:

Mary Lennox	Lisa Burrows
Mr Craven	Richard Walker
Colin	Paul Chisholm
Mrs Medlock	Carole Dance
Martha	Cerianne Roberts
Dickon	Jonathan Williams
Ben Weatherstaff	Richard Walker

Directed by Rosamunde Hutt
Designed by Alex Bunn
Music by Andrew Dodge

CHARACTERS

Major Roles

Mary Lennox, a young girl
Martha, a young maid
Mrs Medlock, housekeeper to Mr Craven
Dickon, Martha's younger brother
Colin, Mr Craven's son
Ben Weatherstaff, a gardener
Mr Craven, Mary's uncle

If required, Mr Craven and Ben Weatherstaff can be
doubled

Minor Roles
To be played by the cast

Photographer
Mother
Father
Ayah
Servant
Ship 1
Ship 2

Animals
Puppets to be operated by cast or stage management

Snake
Robin
Lamb
Fox
Raven

The action of the play takes place in India and then in and
around Misselthwaite Manor in Yorkshire

Time — the early 20th century

AUTHOR'S NOTE

I was commissioned to dramatize Frances Hodgson Burnett's book by Vicky Ireland for Polka Children's Theatre in Wimbledon. The first task I set myself was to make a list of all the ideas this classic story prompted. And the first word that came into my head was "transformation".

As the change from winter to spring brings the garden to life, persuading it to release its secrets, so the characters of Mary and Colin, and finally Mr Craven, begin to bloom. Mary learns to talk to birds, to skip and laugh, to experience the joy of watching things grow. Colin discovers the feel of a new-born lamb, the touch of a bird's feather, and the strength of his own under-used limbs. Mr Craven learns how to release his locked-in grief and open himself once again to the warmth of human contact.

The gardeners of the story — the people who do the tending and nurturing of these characters — are the ordinary plain-speaking no-nonsense characters of Martha, Dickon and Ben Weatherstaff. They provide the key which unlocks the tightly-shut door inside Mary and motivates her, in turn, to bring Colin and his father out of their darkness and into the light.

To Colin and Mary this process of transformation appears so amazing and new that the only word they can think of to describe it is "magic". But to Dickon and Ben it's something much more ordinary — just an everyday aspect of the world they live in. It doesn't bother them that they don't understand the mysteries of nature. They've learned to work with it and love it, and that's enough.

So "transformation" became a key theme in my dramatization of the story. And I wanted this theme to be evident not merely in the text, but in what the audience sees. Consequently, some notion of design became crucial in the writing, and this immediately posed practical problems.

Polka's stage is relatively small. There are no flying facilities, space in the wings is very limited, and there is no army of stage managers ready to rush in the moment the lights dim. Yet the story demands that scenes move rapidly from interior to exterior many times. Also, as the play unfolds, a garden must gradually come into full bloom.

What I didn't want was a lot of clumsy scene changes, with furniture being heaved on and off every few minutes, killing any dramatic build. To avoid this, I opted for a degree of stylization. Alex Bunn, who designed the original production, realized this quite beautifully in his set design, and by using the characters to effect scene changes and changes in the garden, director Rosamunde Hutt made each change a watchable and enjoyable transformation in itself.

The prologue is set in India, which was suggested by long drapes of silk-like material hung so as to give the impression of some sort of outdoor pavilion. At the end of the prologue the material was removed to reveal the main set standing behind it.

Two revolves, operated by the cast, allowed the change from manor house to garden to happen quickly and easily. Furniture was kept to a minimum, and was carefully selected so as to define particular rooms, without the necessity of setting up walls or practical doors.

The journey through the gardens was again highly stylized, achieved by actors visibly moving screens around the stage to give the impression of a complex series of walls and doors. At other times they posed as statues. Music helps enormously in sequences of this nature, as it does in the scene changes.

Once the convention of this sort of stylized theatre is established, operating puppets presents no great problem. It becomes quite acceptable to see the operator, whenever this proves necessary. An audience will take pleasure in clever theatricality.

It's rarely my intention as a playwright to lay down strict guidelines as to how a set should look, what furniture should be used etc. I like to feel I'm leaving enough room within a text for a director and designer to create their own ideas on staging, based on the resources and acting space they have at their disposal. My only advice would be not to attempt any kind of heavy literal design which would be likely to slow down the action and disrupt the rhythm and build of the drama. The story is about using your imagination — so use it.

Neil Duffield

MUSIC

Music recurs throughout the play. It underscores and punctuates the action helping to create and change mood, indicate passage of time, and signal a more stylized form.

The following pieces of music were used in the original production. They are listed here merely as suggestions; directors may choose whatever music they like.

Maurice Ravel
Pavane pour une Infante défunte
Le Tombeau de Couperin
Tzigane
Introduction for harp, flute, clarinet and string quartet
Gaspard de la Nuit

English Traditional Jig
Hunting the Hare

Andrew Dodge

PROLOGUE

Music underscores the whole of the prologue. It should have some Indian influence and a slightly surreal out-of-kilter feel

The Lights come up on Mary Lennox; we are presented with the image of a young girl alone in the world

We are in the India of the British Raj

Mary (*to the audience*) Everyone said Mary Lennox was the most disagreeable child they'd ever come across. It was true too.

A photographer enters with tripod, camera and flashpan

Photographer (*to the audience*) She was a sickly, fretful, ugly, little thing with a thin face and a sour expression. (*He sets up his tripod and camera*)

Mary pouts at the camera as Father enters dressed in imperial uniform

Father (*to the audience*) She had been born and brought up in India, where her father held a position of some importance. (*He stands next to Mary and poses for the camera*)

Mother enters

Mother (*to the audience*) Her mother was a great beauty who loved dancing and parties.(*She poses next to her husband*) She hadn't wanted a little girl at all. (*She snaps her fingers*)

Mary's ayah enters

Mother signals to the ayah to take Mary away

Ayah (*to the audience*) Mary was looked after by an ayah who was told she must keep the child out of sight as much as possible.

The ayah leads Mary, with difficulty, out of the pose. Mary swings a kick at her and just misses

Mary Pig!

The ayah salaams apologetically

The photographer takes his picture; there is a flash. Father and Mother relax and turn to each other, ignoring Mary, who stares sullenly. The photographer packs up his tripod and camera; as he does so we hear a terrible wailing from off stage. Mother and Father exchange anxious looks

   The Photographer exits hurriedly

Mother What is it?
Father I told you we should have gone to the hills!
Mother You never said it had broken out among the servants!
Father (*accusingly*) If it hadn't have been for that stupid dinner party of yours ...

   Father and Mother exit hastily

The ayah begins to back away from Mary. More voices add to the wailing and the music builds

Mary What's happening? Who's making that awful wailing? Tell them to stop! I don't like it! (*To the ayah*) Where are you going?

The ayah continues to back away

   (*Stamping her foot angrily*) Come back here! I'm giving you an order! You're my servant! You have to do what I say!

   The ayah breaks away and runs off

The music and wailing continue to build and distort. There is an atmosphere of rising panic

   A servant rushes on, clearly very ill

   You! What's happening? Tell me what's happening!

The servant hardly spares Mary a glance

   How dare you ignore me? How dare you!

The servant exits

The Photographer rushes across the stage with his camera, ignoring Mary completely

Father hurries in with suitcases

Father, what is it? Why is everyone rushing about?
Father Not now, Mary! Not now!

Father exits

Mother enters with an armful of dresses, following Father and shouting after him

Mother What do I care if they're sick! I want to know who's going to pack my cases!

Mary tries to attract her attention

Mother brushes Mary aside and exits

Mary squats down sulkily and covers her ears. The music and wailing build to a climax. Mary falls asleep and the sounds fade to a soft musical underscore which continues under the following scene. The Lights dim

A small snake (an actor operating a puppet) enters

Snake She did not know what had happened in the house around her. She did not see the bodies of the dead. She had never heard the word "cholera".

Mary wakes and watches the snake

Mary Where is everyone? Why is it so quiet?
Snake Soon others will arrive and find her. One life. One small solitary life amid so much death.

The snake exits

We hear a blast from a ship's siren. The music swells and the lighting changes

Two actors enter and create a ship around Mary

Ship 1 She was to be put on a ship, they decided, and sent back home.
Mary Home? Where's home?
Ship 2 England, of course.
Ship 1 They're sending you to live with your uncle.
Ship 2 Mr Archibald Craven.
Ship 1 In Yorkshire.
Mary But I don't know anything about him!
Ship 2 (*confiding*) Parents are both dead.
Ship 1 She's a plain little piece of goods.
Ship 2 And they say her mother was such a beauty.
Mary I won't listen to you! I won't! I won't! (*She sticks her fingers in her ears*)
Ship 1 (*mocking*) Mary Mary, quite contrary!
Ship 2 How does your garden grow?
Ship 1 How does your garden grow?
Ship 2 How does your garden grow?

The ship's siren blasts

The ship actors exit, laughing

The Lights fade to a spot on Mary standing alone; the music slowly fades to silence. We hear a distant reprise of the wailing. Mary doesn't react to it. The Prologue ends with the same image it began with — a young girl alone in the world

ACT I

Mary remains on stage. The wailing continues softly

The set changes to Mary's bedroom at Misselthwaite Manor and the wailing fades out. The Lights come up

Mrs Medlock and Martha enter

Mrs Medlock and Martha stand for a moment or two, staring at Mary. Mary remains aloof

Mrs Medlock Well. I suppose as you're here, you might as well be told something about the place. Though what they've sent you to Misselthwaite Manor for I can't imagine.

Mary shows no interest

Mrs Medlock and Martha set up Mary's bedroom — a chair and a small table — as Mrs Medlock speaks

It's a gloomy house — there's no other way of describing it — gloomy in more ways than one. Not a place for a child. (*She pauses to see if this has any effect*)

It doesn't

It's very old and it's very big. Six hundred years and nigh on a hundred rooms — though most of them's shut up. There's fine paintings and fine furniture, and outside there's gardens and trees with branches trailing down to the ground — some of them at any rate. But that's it. There's nothing else. Nothing. (*She waits for Mary to react*) Don't you have anything to say?

Mary I know nothing of such places.

Mrs Medlock They said you were a strange one. You look as if you don't even care.

Mary It doesn't make any difference whether I care or not.

Mrs Medlock Well, I don't suppose anyone could argue with that. Did they say anything to you about your uncle?

Mary They said he was my mother's brother.

Mrs Medlock Hmmm. He's another strange one — no point in pretending otherwise … He's not always been that way, mind. Before his wife died you wouldn't have found a man more full of life.

Mary She died?

Mrs Medlock (*softening*) Like a pair of lovebirds they were. She was a beauty — a rare beauty. Folks said the only reason she married him was for his money, but I knew different. They'd have walked the earth for each other those two. This was a different house when she was alive. (*She comes back to reality*) He has a crooked back — not that you're very likely to see him. He sees nobody. And you mustn't expect there'll be people to talk to. You'll just have to look after yourself. You can play in the gardens but here in the house you're not to go poking around.

Mary I shall not want to go poking around.

Mrs Medlock This room is where you'll live — and you're to keep to it.

Mrs Medlock exits

Martha sets out some food during the following. Mary watches her in silence. Martha gives Mary a friendly smile. Mary ignores it

Martha She's not as fierce as she seems — Mrs Medlock. Her heart's in t' right place.

Mary (*looking out of the window*) What's that out there?

Martha You mean the moor?

Mary What's a moor?

Martha Tha' dun't know what a moor is?

Mary Why should I?

Martha I don't suppose they have 'em in India, do they? It's miles and miles of wild land. Does tha' like it?

Mary No. No I hate it.

Martha That's because tha'r not used to it. It just looks big and bare. You will like it though.

Mary Do you?

Martha I love it. It's not really bare. It's covered wi' all sorts o' growing things. In spring and summer when t' gorse an' broom an' heather's in flower, it's like nowt on earth. I wouldn't live away from t' moor for owt.

Mary Why do you talk so strangely?

Martha (*slightly stung*) It's not strange for round here.

Mary What's your name?

Martha (*brightening again*) Martha.

Mary Are you going to be my ayah?

Martha Your what?

Mary My servant.

Martha Mrs Medlock said I was to wait on you a bit … I don't expect tha'll need much waitin' on though, eh?

Mary I shall need someone to dress me.

Martha Can't you do it yourself?

Mary My ayah always did it.

Martha Well I reckon it's time a lass as big as thee learnt to dress herself, don't you?

Mary In India ladies always have servants to dress them.

Martha (*feeling put down*) There's your porridge here, look. It's going cold.

Mary I don't want it.

Martha It's good. Spread a bit of treacle on, or sugar.

Mary I don't want it.

Martha If my brothers and sisters were here they'd polish it off in a twinkling.

Mary Take it to them then. They can have it.

Martha (*offended*) It's not mine to take. And anyway it's not my day off — I only get to see them once a month.

Mary You'll have to throw it away then, won't you?

Martha sides things on to a tray during the following

Martha What are you going to do?

Mary How should I know?

Martha You could go outside if you want.

Mary Why should I do that?

Martha Well there's nowt to do in here.

Martha heads for the exit with the tray, then stops, softening as she becomes aware of Mary's loneliness

You could go and play in t' gardens.

Mary There's no-one to play with.

Martha Play by thi'sen. That's what our Dickon does.

Mary Who's Dickon?

Martha My brother. He meets all his friends out there on t' moor. Birds, sheep, rabbits — they all know our Dickon.

Mary Are there animals out there? (*She looks out of the window*)

Martha smiles, glad to have generated a bit of interest. She reaches for a scarf and wraps it round Mary

Martha Here … If tha' goes round that way, you'll come to t' gardens (*she points*) — over there, look — there's rows of 'em, like a maze, all different. Trees, fountains, pools, statues — there's all sorts. Not any flowers o' course. Not till t' spring.

Mary All I can see are high walls.

Martha They're just to keep wind out. Gardens are inside … You can get in, though. Just walk through from one to t' next. They never bother locking any o' t' doors — except for one.

Mary What do you mean?

Martha One o' t' gardens is kept locked up.

Mary Why?

Martha Nobody's been in it for years.

Mary Is there something wrong with it?

Martha Mr Craven had it shut up when his wife died. It was her garden, they reckon. He locked the door and buried the key.

Mary What for? What made him do that?

A bell rings

Martha That's Mrs Medlock's bell. I'd best run.

Martha exits

Music plays and the Lights change to a non-naturalistic setting. The set changes from the manor house to the garden. The transformation should take place gradually and be stylized to represent a journey; Mary wanders slowly

*around the stage and walls and sections of garden are moved magically
around her so that she passes through a maze of different gardens and
several doors. Now and again she stops to explore some detail or peer at what
to her is an entirely new and strange world. Again we should get an image
of her being entirely alone*

*Finally, when the set transformation is complete, Mary reaches an ivy-
covered wall with no apparent door. She comes to a stop*

The music ends and the Light changes to an outdoor setting

Mary searches for a door in the wall

Mary There must be a door somewhere. All the other walls had one. (*She
tries to peer over the wall*) There's a garden in there. I can see the tops of
trees.

*The robin appears on the wall and sings and hops around during the
following*

(*Watching the robin with interest*) You're a funny little bird. Not like the
birds in India. Is that where you live? Over there? I wish I could see …
What's in there? Is it the secret garden — the one that's kept locked — the
one nobody's allowed in? (*She watches the bird as it sings away*)

Ben Weatherstaff enters

Ben Well I'll be danged!

The robin flutters over to him and continues moving around

Tha's made thi'sen a friend, I see.
Mary Why does it come to you like that?
Ben I've knowed this little fella since he were a fledgling. He's al'us nosing
about. … Sithi. He knows we're talking about him.
Mary What kind of a bird is it?
Ben Dun't tha' know a robin redbreast when tha' sees one? They're t'
friendliest birds alive, are robins … He's a bit lonely though, is this one.
He could do wi' a mate.
Mary (*watching as the robin hops around*) I'm lonely.
Ben Tha'rt little wench from India, aren't tha'?
Mary Yes.
Ben No wonder tha'r lonely. Tha'll be lonelier still afore tha's done.

Mary What's your name?
Ben Ben Weatherstaff … I'm a bit lonely mi'sen if truth be known. Yon'
robin's best friend I've got.
Mary I don't have any friends. I never had. My ayah didn't like me one bit.
Ben We must be wove out o' t' same cloth then. Both as sour as we look.

The robin sings

Mary I wish I knew what it was saying.
Ben He's made his mind up to make friends wi' thi.
Mary With me? Do you want to make friends, little robin? Would you?

The robin approaches Mary

Ben He likes thi, see.
Mary Does he? (*To the robin*) I like you too.
Ben Tha' knows how to talk to him all right — like young Dickon.
Mary You know Dickon?
Ben Everybody knows Dickon. Creatures more than folk. There's nowt
much about wild things as Dickon can't tell you.

The robin flies over the wall

Mary He's gone back into the garden!
Ben That's where he lives. Over in t' rose trees.
Mary Are there rose trees in there?
Ben 'Appen. Who knows? (*He decides enough's been said and busies
himself with some work*)
Mary I want to have a look inside that garden.
Ben Well you can't. There's no way in.
Mary There must be a door somewhere.
Ben There were ten year ago, but there isn't now.
Mary But there must be! There has to be! Show me where it is!
Ben There's none as anyone can find, and none as is anyone's business. Now
get you gone and play. There's work to be done.

Ben exits

*Music plays; the lights change.The set changes around Mary, becoming her
room in the manor house again*

It is late evening. Mary sits reading

Martha enters

The music fades out; we hear the distant wailing. Martha pretends not to hear it

Mary What was that?
Martha What was what?
Mary That wailing sound. You heard it.
Martha The wind, that's all. You'd bare stand up if you were out on t' moor tonight.
Mary It sounded like ——
Martha Like what?
Mary — something I once heard in India.
Martha It's a funny thing — imagination.

More wailing

Mary That's not imagination! It's real! It's here! In the house! Down one of those corridors! (*She heads for the exit*)

Mrs Medlock enters in a fluster

Mrs Medlock And where do you think you're going?
Mary I heard a wailing sound. Someone crying.
Mrs Medlock You heard nothing of the sort, and if you set foot down those corridors, young madam, you'll get your ears well and truly boxed!

Mrs Medlock leads Mary back into the room

Now stay where you're told or you'll find yourself locked up! I've enough on my plate without having to deal with your moithering!
Martha Do you need any help, ma'am?
Mrs Medlock Just make sure she stays put.

Mrs Medlock exits

Mary (*angry and hurt*) There *was* someone crying! There *was*! I know there was! I heard it!

Martha waits for Mary to settle a bit

Martha I didn't get chance to say owt before: I've brought some'at for thi.
Mary What?

Martha produces a skipping rope and gives it to Mary

Martha A pedlar came to t' door selling pots and pans. It were only tuppence.
He had 'em wi' blue handles — I've al'us liked red though.
Mary (*examining the skipping rope*) What is it?
Martha Don't they have skipping ropes in India?

Mary looks blank

Here. Let me show thi.

Martha takes back the rope and skips

>   Teddy on the railway
>   Picking up stones
>   Along came an engine
>   And broke Teddy's bones
>   "Oh," said Teddy, "that's not fair."
>   "Oh," said the engine, "I don't care!"
(*She finishes skipping*) I could skip every rhyme in t' book when I were
your age – wi'out stopping. Here — have a try.
Mary What for?
Martha What for? For fun. It's for fun.
Mary I don't know the words.
Martha That dun't matter. I'll say them … Here.

Mary takes the rope and tries to skip

Martha   Teddy on the ——

Mary fails

Try again.
>   Teddy on the ——

Mary fails

Mary Ahrrr!
Martha It takes a bit of practice, that's all … Go on. Do it again.

Mary manages a skip

>   Teddy on the railway ——

Mary I did one!
Martha   Picking up ——

Mary fails

See! I told you! You have to keep at it, that's all.
Mary Is this a present?
Martha If tha' wants to call it that.
Mary Thank you. (*She holds out her hand*)
Martha (*shaking Mary's hand*) Tha're a queer little thing and no mistake.
If it'd been our Ellen she'd have give us a kiss.
Mary Do you want me to kiss you?
Martha No … If tha' were different, p'rps tha'd want to.

There is a pause

Mary   (*deciding to take a risk*) I found that garden — the one no-one's
allowed into.
Martha I knew tha'd not be able to stop thinking about it; I were t' same when
they first told me.
Mary There isn't even a door any more – I looked all round. Why did my
uncle shut it up?
Martha (*making a decision to confide in Mary*) The way it were told to me,
it were like their special place — her and him — when they were first
married. They did all t' gardening 'emselves. They'd go inside and shut the
door and stay there for hours, planting things in t' ground and talking and
laughing wi' each other. She loved flowers, that's what Mrs Medlock al'us
says, roses especially … You mustn't ever say I told you.

Mary shakes her head

There was this tree. Old and twisted and dead. Not a leaf on it. So she trained
some o' t' roses to grow over it — bringing it back to life, sort of thing. They
say it were a picture in summer. And it had a branch, bent like a seat, that
she used to sit on … Well, one day the branch broke. She fell to t' ground
and were hurt that bad … Well, next day she died.
Mary Is that why he hates the garden? Does he think it killed her?
Martha He locked it up and wouldn't hear mention of it. Mrs Medlock
reckons he locked up all his feelings wi' t' same key.
Mary I've made friends with someone who lives in that garden.
Martha You've what?
Mary A robin … He flew over the wall.
Martha So you did find yourself a playmate after all? I knew tha' would —
same as our Dickon.

Mary I like your Dickon. I've never seen him, but I think I like him.
Martha Everybody likes Dickon. I wonder what he'd make o' thee?
Mary He wouldn't like me.
Martha What makes you say that?
Mary No-one ever does.
Martha How do you like yourself?
Mary Not at all really.
Martha Why don't you practise your rope a bit?

Martha exits

The Lights change

Music plays, softly underscoring the following

Mary teaches herself to skip during the following. The set is changed around her, recreating the gardens and the ivy-covered wall

Mary   Teddy on the ——
                           (*She fails and starts again*)
                           Teddy on the railway
                           Picking up ——
                           (*She fails and starts again*)
                           Teddy on the railway
                           Picking up stones
                           Along came an ——
                           (*She fails and starts again*)

Ben Weatherstaff enters and watches Mary

                           Teddy on the railway
                           Picking up stones
                           Along came an engine
                           And broke Teddy's bones
                           "Oh," said the engine, "that's not ——"
                           (*She fails*)

By now Mary and Ben are in the garden. The music fades out and the Lights come up to an outdoor state

Ben Well, I'll be danged. Happen tha'r a young 'un after all.
Mary I'm not very good. I haven't got to the end of the rhyme once yet.
Ben Well, tha's skipped some red into thi cheeks or my name's not Ben
  Weatherstaff.

The robin enters

Mary (*watching the robin*) Does he remember me, do you think?
Ben Remembers thi? He knows every cabbage stump in t' garden. If owt new
stirs round here tha' can be sure that little feller knows about it.
Mary Is anything new stirring in that garden?
Ben (*suddenly surly*) What garden?
Mary You said there were rose trees over there. Are they all dead?
Ben Ask him. He's th'only one as can answer that. N'b'dy else has been
inside for ten year. (*He heads away*)
Mary Wait! Come back! I'm ordering you!

Ben exits

Mary (*to the robin*) I wish you could talk to me. I wish you could tell me what
it's like over there. I do hope it's not all dead.

The robin flutters away a little

(*Following the robin*) If I had wings like yours, I'd fly with you over the
wall to see.

*The robin flutters away again. Mary follows. The robin hops around on the
ground, singing away*

What are you after? A worm, is it? Here — let me help. (*She puts her hand
into the earth*) There's something here … But it's not a worm. (*She draws
out a key*) A key! (*To the robin*) You knew this was there, didn't you? You
wanted me to find it. You were leading me to it! Is it the key to the secret
garden? Is this where my uncle buried it all those years ago?

The robin flies away again, still singing

What is it now? Something else you want to show me? What? What is it?

The robin alights on the ivy which covers the wall

Mary Something in the ivy? (*She reaches into the foliage and gropes
around*) Something round … A knob — a door knob! (*She feels around
further*) And a keyhole! (*She takes the key*) Will it fit? Oh please make it
fit! Please! (*She puts the key into the hole*) It's turning! It's unlocking! (*She
steps back, glances around, takes a deep breath and pushes the door*)

Music plays and the Lights change to a magical state. The ivy wall is removed slowly and the secret garden is revealed

Mary passes into the garden

The Lights return to the outdoor state

Mary stands for a few moments, just gazing

The music fades out

Mary How still it is. How very very still.

The robin joins her

It looks dead. Is it, robin? You know everything about the garden. Is everything dead?

The robin flutters to the ground and starts to sing, as if showing Mary something else

(*Moving to look*) Shoots. Green shoots! But so tiny — pushing and struggling out of the earth. Will they be flowers? They're alive, whatever they are. So it's not all dead! I'll clear away some of this grass so they can breathe!

Music plays

Mary starts work. She moves from flower bed to flower bed, weeding and digging

The ivy wall is moved back into position, hiding Mary's activities. The Lights cross-fade to the exterior of the wall and the music fades out

Dickon appears in front of the wall and starts to play a wooden pipe

Various animals appear, drawn by the music

Mary, similarly drawn, emerges through the ivy-wall behind Dickon. She moves round until he sees her, then stops

Dickon stops playing the pipe

Dickon Move gentle. Else tha'll startle 'em.

Mary remains motionless

  The animals gradually exit

Mary I once saw someone charm a snake playing music like that.
Dickon Tha'r Miss Mary, aren't tha?
Mary I know who you are too. You're Dickon.

The robin comes over to her

Dickon Tha's made friends already I see.
Mary He's Ben Weatherstaff's friend really, but I think he knows me a little
  bit.
Dickon He wouldn't come near if he didn't. He'll tell me all about thi in a
  minute.
Mary Can you understand what he says?
Dickon It's not hard. Not if tha listens right.
Mary Ben Weatherstaff says you know all about wild things.
Dickon He al'us says I should've been born a creature.
Mary What about gardens?
Dickon Gardens?
Mary Do you know about gardens — gardens that have gone wild?
Dickon Why? Does tha know o' one?
Mary Could you keep a secret? A very important secret?
Dickon I keep secrets all t' time. Birds' nests, rabbit warrens, fox holes.
  There wouldn't be a creature safe on t' moor if I couldn't keep a secret.
Mary I've stolen a garden.
Dickon Tha's what?
Mary Nobody wants it. Nobody ever goes in it. I've nothing to do, you see.
  Nothing belongs to me. Nothing at all … The robin showed me how to get
  in.
Dickon Where is it?
Mary I'd die if anyone ever found out!
Dickon They'll not from me.

Mary decides to show Dickon the garden. She leads him through the ivy wall

Music plays and the lighting changes. The wall is moved away

Dickon and Mary stand inside the secret garden. Dickon is spellbound

The music ends

Mary It's a secret garden and I'm the only one in the world who wants it to come alive.

Dickon I never thought I'd see inside this place.

Mary You mean you knew about it?

Dickon Martha told me there was one as nobody ever went in.

Mary Ben said there were rose trees here. But I think they might all be dead.

Dickon Not them. Not all of 'em, any road. (*He takes out a penknife and cuts into the stem of one of the rose trees*) See — (*he shows the stem to Mary*) green in t' middle.

Mary Does that mean it's alive?

Dickon It's as wick as thee and me.

Mary Wick? Wick. Oh that's a lovely word. Wick! It's wick! Oh Dickon, I'm so glad it's wick! I want them all to be wick! Let's have a look and see how many are wick!

Dickon laughs and cuts into more of the rose trees

Wick! Wick ! Wick!

Dickon They've run wild all right. Spread till they're a wonder! There'll be a fountain o' roses here this summer! (*He discovers some of Mary's handiwork*) What's this? Who's done this?

Mary Have I done wrong? I didn't know what they were — they looked so fragile. It seemed like they were being strangled. I've not killed them, have I?

Dickon Killed 'em? A trained gardener couldn't have done better. You watch — them bulbs'll shoot up.

Mary What are bulbs?

Dickon They're down there — under t' ground, working away like fury, pushing up their little green points ready for t' spring.

Mary Will they become flowers?

Dickon All over — daffodils, lilies, snowdrops ... Tha's done a lot, hasn't tha — for a little wench.

Mary I'm getting stronger. I ate some of Martha's porridge this morning.

Dickon Tha'll need it an'all. There's some work needs doin' in here.

Mary Will you help me? Will you teach me, Dickon? I can dig and pull up weeds. I'll do whatever you tell me.

Dickon I were hopin' tha'd ask. I'll come every day if tha wants! This is 't best fun I've had in ages! I wouldn't want us to make it into a gardener's garden mind — all spick and span. I like it more like this — running wild.

Mary It wouldn't seem like a secret garden if we made it all neat and tidy.

Dickon A secret garden? It's that right enough ... All t' same, I reckon someone's been in since it were first shut up.

Mary How could they? The door was locked and the key buried. I only found it today.

Dickon Maybe – but there's been a bit o' pruning done. More recent than ten year ago an' all.

Mary Who could have done it?

Dickon Don't ask me … Happen yon little chap! (*He indicates the robin*)

Mary (*laughing*) Will we be able to plant flowers of our own as well?

Dickon What sort would tha like?

Mary Are there any that look like bells?

Dickon Silver bells and cockle shells? Mary Mary, quite contrary ——

Mary They used to call me that.

Dickon Tha' dun't seem contrary to me.

Mary I like you, Dickon — and that makes four.

Dickon Four?

Mary Four people I like. Martha, Ben Weatherstaff, the robin — and you.

Dickon Well I thought I were a rum 'un, but tha' must be t'rummest ever.

Mary (*trying out the accent*) Does tha like me though?

Dickon (*laughing*) Ay. I reckon I do — and that makes two o'n us.

Mary Two?

Dickon Me and t' robin.

Mary Two for me! Two for Contrary Mary! ... You wouldn't tell anyone? About the garden. You'd never tell?

Dickon If tha were yon little robin and tha'd just showed me thi nest, does tha' think I'd tell? Thi secret's as safe as that robin's.

Music plays and the lighting changes

    Dickon exits

Mary sits alone with her thoughts

The set is changed to a room in the manor

    Mrs Medlock enters and paces impatiently

Mary gets up and runs to Mrs Medlock

The music ends

Mrs Medlock At last! Where on earth have you been?

Mary In the gardens.

Mrs Medlock I've had Martha searching all over — and look at the state of you! You look like you've been pulled through an hedge backwards! Heaven knows what Mr Craven's going to think!

Mary My uncle? But I thought you said he never ——

Mrs Medlock He's asked to see you. He's going abroad and he wants to speak to you before he leaves ... For goodness' sake straighten yourself up a bit.

Mrs Medlock tidies Mary's dress

Mr Craven enters

Mrs Medlock takes Mary across to Mr Craven

Mrs Medlock She's here, sir ... This is Miss Mary.
Mr Craven You may leave her here, Mrs Medlock. I'll ring when I want you to take her away.

Mrs Medlock exits

Pause

(*Looking at Mary*) Are you well?
Mary Yes.
Mr Craven Do they take good care of you?
Mary Yes.
Mr Craven You're very thin.
Mary I'm getting fatter.
Mr Craven Where do you play?
Mary (*guardedly*) Everywhere. Martha gave me a skipping rope. I'm getting quite good. I can nearly get to the end of the rhyme. I don't do any harm.
Mr Craven Harm? Of course you don't do any harm. You're a child, what harm could you possibly do? You may do whatever you like.
Mary May I?
Mr Craven Of course. I shall be travelling in Europe for the summer. Mrs Medlock is to see you have whatever you need. Is there anything you'd like? Toys? Books?
Mary (*after a hesitation*) There is something.
Mr Craven Speak up then. What is it?
Mary Might I have a bit of earth?
Mr Craven Earth?
Mary To plant seeds in — to make things grow.
Mr Craven You like gardening, do you?
Mary I didn't know about gardens in India. I didn't understand about them, you see. But it's different here. I want to watch things come alive.
Mr Craven You put me in mind of someone. Someone else who loved making things come alive.

Mary I'm only starting. I've got a lot to learn.

Mr Craven You can have as much earth as you want.

Mary May I take it from anywhere — if it's not wanted, I mean?

Mr Craven Anywhere. Take it from anywhere. Anywhere at all.

Mary Thank you … Thank you very much.

Mr Craven You must go now. I won't see you again until the autumn. (*He rings a bell*)

Mrs Medlock enters

I've spoken with the child. Let her run wild in the garden. Don't look after her too much.

Mrs Medlock No, sir. I won't.

Mr Craven and Mrs Medlock exit

Mary I can have my garden! I can have my garden!

Music plays and the Lighting changes to night-time shadows

Mary's room is set up

Mary settles herself in her room

Martha enters and busies herself around the room, then gazes out of the window

The music continues under the following dialogue

Martha It's a wild night. Look at the rain.

We hear the distant wailing. Mary gives Martha a demanding look

I swear that wind'll bring them chimneys down one o' these days.

More wailing

It's nothing to fret about. 'Night.

Martha hurries out, anxious to avoid questions

There is more wailing and the music continues to underscore the action

Mary That isn't the wind! It's someone crying. Crying like they did in India!
   I don't care what Mrs Medlock says, I'm going to find out who's doing it!
   (*She lights a candle and sets off into the darkness*)

*There follows a stylized journey along the corridors underscored by music
and wailing*

   This way? Or that? I've never seen so many corridors.

*Mary moves around the acting area. As she does so, various things appear
which she examines in candle-light: a painting, a statue, a tapestry — and
finally a door. She pushes the door open and steps through*

*The music ends and a dim Light comes up on Colin's room, a feature of which
is a cord hanging down*

   Colin is sitting in a bath chair, crying

Mary stares at Colin. He notices her and stops crying

Colin Are you a ghost?
Mary No. Are you?
Colin No.
Mary Who are you?
Colin Colin.
Mary Who's Colin?
Colin Colin Craven. Who are you?
Mary Mary Lennox. Mr Craven is my uncle.
Colin He's my father.
Mary Your father? No-one ever told me he had a son!
Colin We must be cousins.
Mary Yes. Did no-one tell you I'd come to live here?
Colin No. They wouldn't. None of them would dare.
Mary Why not?
Colin Because I never let anyone see me ... They always talk about me. They
   tell each other I won't live to grow up. I won't have people talking about
   me!
Mary What a strange house this is. Everything's locked up and hidden away.
Colin I'm not locked up. I stay in my room because I want to.
Mary Does your father come and see you?
Colin Sometimes. Usually when I'm asleep. He doesn't like seeing me
   though. I think he hates me.

Mary Why?

Colin Because my mother died when I was born.

Mary She died when you were born? Then that means you must have been born just after she —— (*She stops herself*)

Colin Just after she what?

Mary I think he hates the garden for the same reason.

Colin What garden?

Mary You don't even know about it?

Colin No. What is it? Tell me.

Mary (*changing the subject*) Do you always sit in that chair?

Colin I have to. I'm ill. I've always been ill. They used to put an iron thing on my back, but a big doctor came from London and made them take it off. He said they should take me out in the fresh air instead. I won't let them, though. I hate going outside. Everyone looks at me.

Mary I'll go away if you like.

Colin No ... No, I want to talk to you. I want to know about that garden.

Mary (*deciding to tell him*) It's one your mother used to like — her favourite ... She made it with your father. They used to go in together. It was their special place.

Colin Nobody's ever told me about this.

Mary After she died he locked it up.

Colin Why? What made him to that?

Mary I'm not sure — no-one will talk about it ... I think they've been told not to answer questions.

Colin I could *make* them answer. They have to do what I say. They all know that. I could *make* them tell us about it!

Mary (*hurriedly*) Why do people say you won't live to grow up?

Colin Because it's true. People have always said that. Ever since I was born.

Mary Did the big doctor from London say it?

Colin No — no, not him.

Mary What did he say?

Colin He said I might live if I made my mind up to. He said they had to try and put me in the right sort of humour.

Mary I know someone who could put you in the right sort of humour!

Colin Who?

Mary Dickon!

Colin What a queer name. Is it a boy?

Mary You don't know him? I thought everyone knew Dickon. He charms animals — foxes and squirrels and birds.

Colin You mean he makes magic?

Mary He doesn't call it magic. He plays music and they all come to listen. He can even talk to them. He's like a wood fairy. Dickon could make you feel better, I know he could!

Colin An animal charmer ... I could be a boy animal!

They both laugh

That garden. That locked-up garden that used to be my mother's. That would make me feel better too ... I want to see it, Mary. I'll make them unlock it. I'll make them take us inside!

Mary Oh no! Please, you mustn't do that — you mustn't!

Colin Why not? Don't you want to see it too?

Mary Yes ... Yes, I do. But don't you see? If you make them open the door you'll spoil it! It won't be a secret any more!

Colin A secret?

Mary You see ... You see, if there were a door, hidden somewhere under the ivy, and we could find it and slip through and shut it behind us, then no-one would know we were inside — it would be our secret! We could plant seeds in the ground and make it all come alive again!

Colin I never had a secret before.

Mary If I look hard I might be able to find the key. And there must be a door somewhere. I could ask Dickon to push you there without anyone seeing us. Then it would be ours — just the three of us!

Colin I should like that, Mary. I should really like that. Our own secret garden. (*He indicates the cord*) You see that cord?

Mary Yes.

Colin Pull it.

Mary pulls the cord. A portrait of a young woman appears

Mary It's your mother, isn't it.

Colin I wish she hadn't died. If she'd lived, maybe my father wouldn't hate me so much.

Mary Her eyes are the same as yours.

Colin Put her away again.

Mary pulls the cord and the portrait disappears

Mary Why do you keep her covered up?

Colin She smiles too much. Besides, she's mine. I don't want everyone to see her.

Mrs Medlock enters

Mrs Medlock Merciful heavens! What's going on here ! (*To Mary*) You! What on earth are you doing in here?

Colin This is my cousin, Mary Lennox. She's come to talk to me.

Mrs Medlock Who let you in? Who told you about ——

Colin Nobody told her anything. She heard me crying and came to find me. Stop getting yourself in such a frenzy.

Mrs Medlock I'm only thinking of you, Master Colin … You mustn't forget how ill you are.

Colin I want to forget how ill I am! Mary makes me forget! I like her. She's to come and talk to me every day.

Mrs Medlock I don't think I could approve of that.

Colin You don't have to approve of anything. Just do as you're told. Now go away and leave us alone.

Mrs Medlock Master Colin, I really don't think ——

Colin Didn't you hear? I said go away!

Mrs Medlock exits

Why are you looking at me like that?

Mary Once when I was in India I saw a boy who was a rajah. He had rubies and emeralds stuck all over him. He spoke to his people the same way you spoke to Mrs Medlock.

Colin They're always trying to make me do things I don't like. I'm glad you came. I want you to come every day.

Mary I'll come when I can but I shall have to go out and look for a way into the garden.

Colin Yes. Of course. You must do that. Do you know Martha?

Mary Yes. I know her well.

Colin I shall tell Martha when you are to come here.

Mary You mean Martha's known about you all the time?

Colin Of course. They all know about me.

Mary I'd better go. Mrs Medlock will be fuming.

Colin I wish I could go to sleep before you leave.

Mary (*after a pause*) When I couldn't sleep my ayah used to stroke my hand. Shut your eyes.

Music plays. Mary takes Colin's hand and strokes it

The Lights fade slowly to black

CURTAIN

ACT II

The secret garden

Music plays. The Lights come up

Mary and Dickon are busily working in the secret garden

The music fades out

Mary It's all so different. Everywhere you look there seem to be buds and shoots – sticking up and sprouting and uncurling.

Dickon It'll look even more different soon. There'll be apple and cherry blossom up there. And peach and plum against the walls. Tha'r starting to look a bit different thi'sen.

Mary (*pleased*) I'm getting fatter. Mrs Medlock said she'll soon have to buy me some new dresses.

Dickon It's fresh air doin' it. Tha'll be tough as a white-thorn knobstick afore long.

Mary (*laughing*) Dickon — there's something I've been wanting to tell you.

Dickon Not another secret?

Mary I'm not sure … Do you know about Colin?

Dickon (*guardedly*) What's tha' know about him?

Mary He keeps asking me to go and talk to him. I've been every day this week. I tell him stories — about the robin and the gardens and when I lived in India.

Dickon Mr Craven dun't like anybody speaking about him.

Mary Does he hate him?

Dickon I wouldn't say that. They reckon he can't stand to look into Colin's eyes though — they remind him too much of hers.

Mary Colin was born just after his mother fell out of that tree. I don't think anybody's told him about that though. He seems to think it was because of him she died.

Dickon No wonder he thinks his father hates him.

Mary He keeps telling me he's going to die … What's wrong with him, Dickon?

Dickon Nobody knows for sure. I think they're worried his back'll grow bent — same as his father's. That's why they al'us push him round in a chair instead o' letting him walk.

Mary There's no sign of his back being bent. And even if there were, it's no
reason to spend all his life shut away in a dark room. A bent back never
stopped his father making this garden!

Dickon You're right. No wonder t' lad's sickly — anybody would be, locked
away like that all t' time.

Mary I've been wondering … Well, if we were to get him to come out here
— into the garden with us — he might be too busy watching things grow
to worry about being ill … He'd have to be able to keep a secret — and I'm
not sure how we'd get him here without anyone seeing.

Dickon He could order all t' servants and gardeners to stay away; they all
have to do as he says. Then we could take him wherever we wanted.

Mary It'd do him good. I know it would. The big doctor from London said
he had to get out into the fresh air more.

Dickon He's like a plant wi' no light. We mun' get him into t' garden, Mary
— watchin' and listenin' and sniffin' and soaked through wi' sunshine!

Mary Ay, that we mun'!

They both laugh

(*Continuing with the accent, pleased with herself*) I tell thi what. When I
go back I'll ask if tha can come and see him. Bring all thi creatures too —
he'll like that. Then we'll fetch him out here and show him t' garden!

Dickon (*laughing*) Tha' should talk a bit o' Yorkshire to him! That'd put a
smile on his face!

Mary I shall talk Yorkshire to him this very day!

Music plays. The Lighting changes

Dickon and Mary exit

Colin screams and wails off stage

The set is changed to the hall in Misselthwaite Manor. As this happens:

Martha enters

Mary enters from the opposite side

The music fades

Martha Miss Mary, wherever has tha' been? We've been searching all over
for you!

Mary Why? What's the matter?

Martha He's gone into one o' his tantrums! We've had a right to-do all
afternoon trying to keep him quiet. Nobody can do owt wi' him!

The screaming continues

Mary He's the most spoilt boy in the world! Someone ought to make him
stop!

Martha He's working himself into hysterics. He keeps asking for you. I
don't know what tha's been saying to him but he won't let anyone else near
him!

Mary Bring him here. Bring him here at once!

*Martha exits and returns, pushing Colin, a cover over his legs, still
screaming*

Stop that screaming! Didn't you hear me? I said stop it at once! I hate you!
Everybody hates you! I wish everyone would run out of the house and let
you scream yourself to death! You *will* scream yourself to death if you go
on like this and we'll all be very glad!!

Colin tries to stop, gasping and choking and spluttering

If you scream one more scream, I shall scream too! And I can scream a lot
louder than you! It'll frighten you! It will! It'll frighten you to death!

Colin (*gulping and sobbing*) I can't stop! I can't help it!

Mary Yes you can! There's nothing wrong with you at all! Nothing except
hysterics! Hysterics and bad temper!

Colin There is something wrong with me! I felt a lump on my back!

Mary No you didn't! There's nothing at all wrong with your horrid back!

Colin Yes there is! I felt it! I felt a lump!

Mary Martha! Martha, come here! Show me his back!

Martha I don't think he'll let me, miss.

Colin Show her! Show her — then she'll see!

Martha reveals Colin's back. Mary examines it

Mary There you are! Not one single lump! Not even a pimple! And if you
ever say there is again I shall laugh at you!

Colin looks to Martha

Martha It's true, Master Colin. There's nowt there.

Mary And even if there were it's no excuse for behaving like this! Plenty of people have things wrong with their back and they don't go round having hysterics about it!

Colin (*fighting back sobs and wounded pride*) Where have you been? Why didn't you come and see me?

Mary If you create a fuss like this I shall never come to see you again!

Colin You'll have to if I say so!

Mary Oh I will, will I?

Colin I'll make you! I'll make them drag you in to see me!

Mary Oh will you, Mr Rajah? Well if you do, I'll sit and clench my teeth and never say a single word to you. I won't even look at you.

Colin Why are you being so selfish?

Mary You're the one who's selfish. You're the most selfish boy I ever saw!

Colin Stop being so horrible! I'm not selfish, I'm ill. I'm very ill and I'm going to die!

Mary I don't believe a word of it! You're not going to die, you just tell people that to try and make them feel sorry for you! I don't think there's anything wrong with you at all! Tha're just a mardy little nowt!

Colin What did you say?

Mary It's about time tha' stopped all this whinging and feeling sorry for thi'sen and got outside into t' fresh air!

Colin What are you talking like that for? You sound like a common cottage girl.

Mary I'd sooner sound like a common cottage girl than a palace rajah! And thee a Yorkshire lad born and bred — tha' should be ashamed o' thi'sen!

There is a pause. Colin is so stunned that he eventually starts to laugh. His laughter infects Mary. Martha picks it up too. All three enjoy laughing together

Martha I can't believe it! A lass like thee talkin' broad Yorkshire!

Mary I'm learning it like French.

Martha Well, it's a blessing on t' lot of us. Tha's cast a spell on him and no mistake.

Mary I can't do magic. I heard about people in India who could, but I don't know how.

Martha Oh I think tha' does. He's met his match wi' thee all right. Tha'r t' best thing that could've happened to him.

Martha exits laughing

Colin I was angry because you hadn't come to see me. I'm sorry.

Mary So you should be. But now you've apologized I can tell you about Dickon.

Colin Is he coming?

Mary Yes. Tomorrow. And he's bringing some of his creatures!

Colin Here! Into the manor? How will he get them to come?

Mary He'll talk to them.

Colin And they understand?

Mary Dickon says any creature will understand if you make friends with it first. But you have to be friends for sure.

Colin I wish I could be friends with things. I never had any friends.

Mary You can be friends with me if you like.

Colin Can I?

Mary I didn't used to have any friends. Ben Weatherstaff said it was because I was as nowty as him. I think you must be like that too. We're all three the same. I don't think I'm as bad as I used to be though.

Colin Did you used to feel as if you hated everyone?

Mary Yes. I would have hated you if I hadn't met the robin and Dickon first.

Colin I'm glad Dickon's coming. I don't mind him looking at me.

Mary There's something else I have to tell you.

Colin What? What is it?

Mary Can I trust you? Can I trust you for sure?

Colin Yes — yes, of course you can!

Mary There *is* a door into the secret garden.

Colin You mean you've found it?

Mary It's hidden under the ivy.

Colin Does that mean I'll be able to see it? Shall I go inside? Shall I really live to go inside?

Mary Of course you'll live to go inside! Why do you always have to say silly things like that? The roses have climbed everywhere — over branches and walls, across the ground. All the greyness is turning to green. It's so still. So safe and still.

Colin You've been in. You've seen inside!

Mary I'd seen inside the first time I met you. I'd found the key and opened the door. I daren't tell you then; I didn't know if I could trust you — not for sure.

Colin Can you trust me for sure now?

Mary Yes. Yes I think I can. I'll see you tomorrow.

Mary exits

Music plays. The Lighting changes

Colin's room is set up

The music ends

Mrs Medlock enters and busies herself around the room

Colin Why doesn't she come? Where is she?

Mrs Medlock I couldn't tell you, Master Colin. Off in them gardens more than likely — and the longer she stops there the better.

Colin I may be going out there myself today.

Mrs Medlock I beg your pardon ...

Colin If the weather's fine.

Mrs Medlock I don't think that's a very good idea. You're not a well child, remember.

Colin I told you before — I don't want to remember!

Mrs Medlock When you've been out before, it hasn't suited you – you know that. It upsets you.

Colin That's when I've been by myself. My cousin Mary will be going with me this time — and a very strong boy.

Mrs Medlock Boy? What boy? Who is he? What's his name?

Colin His name is Dickon.

Mrs Medlock Martha's brother?

Colin He's an animal charmer and he can do magic and he's bringing some of his creatures.

Mrs Medlock Creatures? Here? In the house?

Colin You're to bring them upstairs as soon as they arrive — and you're not to go playing with any of the animals before I've seen them!

Mrs Medlock This is her doing, isn't it? She's arranged all this.

Mary runs in

Mary Colin! Colin, it's here! Oh you never saw anything so beautiful in all your life! I thought it had come the other morning. But it's here for sure now!

Colin What? What's here?

Mary The spring! It's arrived! It's outside! Oh you should see it! It's the most beautiful thing in the world!

Colin Show me, I want to see it! Now! Straight away! Medlock! Open the window!

Mrs Medlock I beg your pardon?

Colin The window! Open the window!

Mrs Medlock But you've never had the window open. Never in your entire life!

Colin Well I want it open now! Open it at once! I want the spring to come inside!

Mrs Medlock Bewitched ... She's bewitched him.

Mrs Medlock opens the window and then exits

Mary Breathe it in. Let the spring into your body. Dickon says it will make
   you live for ever and ever and ever.
Colin (*breathing in*) For ever and ever and ever. He's coming, isn't he? He
   hasn't changed his mind?
Mary Listen! Do you hear anything?

A lamb bleats off stage

Colin What is it?

   Mrs Medlock enters

Mrs Medlock If you please, Master Colin — Dickon … and his "creatures".

   Dickon enters carrying a lamb and accompanied by a fox and a raven

*Colin is speechless with wonder. Dickon walks over to Colin and the lamb
starts nuzzling into Colin's jacket*

Colin What's it doing? What does it want?
Dickon He wants feedin' … Tha' can do it if tha' wants.
Colin Me?

*Dickon pulls a feeding-bottle from his pocket and hands it to Colin. The lamb
suckles ravenously*

   It's eating!
Dickon I found him up on t' moor frozen wi' cold. His mother were dead.
   I wrapped him in my jacket and brought him home.
Colin I've never been near a lamb before.
Dickon Well tha'r not doin' bad. He's takin' a shine to thi.

Colin enjoys feeding the lamb

Colin Medlock — I shall be going out into the gardens with Dickon and my
   cousin and no-one is to come near. You must tell everyone they've got to
   keep right away.
Mrs Medlock Master Colin, I think it would be better if one of the footmen
   stayed with you.
Colin Well I don't. Mary, what was it you told me that Indian rajah used to
   say when he'd finished talking to people?
Mary You have my permission to go.
Colin Medlock — you have my permission to go.

Mrs Medlock exits in a huff

Colin It'll be safe to go in a minute ... Then I shall see it! I shall really see
  it!

*Music plays and the Lights change. During the following, the set changes
around the children, ending with them facing the ivy wall*

*Dickon pushes the bath chair. We follow Dickon, Colin and Mary on a
stylized journey through the gardens. They laugh and Dickon and Mary
enjoy pointing out things to Colin. They come to a halt in front of the ivy wall.
The music continues softly under the following scene*

Mary We're here ... This is it.
Colin Where? I can't see anything.
Mary Nor could I. But just in here, there's a handle — and now — a door!
Colin I can scarcely breathe! (*He covers his eyes*)

*The music swells and the wall is moved away. The secret garden is now much
greener, with splashes of colour around*

The music fades out

Colin (*uncovering his eyes and staring*) It's like Magic. It's like real Magic.
  I shall get well, Mary. I shall.
Dickon Course tha' will. Tha'll live for ever and ever and ever.
Colin Will I? Does tha' really think so?

They all laugh

  (*Peering round*) It's alive, isn't it. It's all alive.
Mary It's as wick as thee and me. Look ... Buds — starting to open. Leaves
  uncurling.
Dickon Snowdrops — daffodils.
Mary (*picking up a feather*) A bird's feather.
Colin Give it to me! I want it! I want to touch it!

Mary hands Colin the feather

  Soft.
Dickon Off a young chaffinch.
Colin Where's the robin? I want to see the robin!
Dickon He'll not be far away. Tha'll see him all right.

Colin (*gazing round, enjoying it all*) That's a very old tree.
Dickon Yes. Yes, it is.

Dickon and Mary exchange a glance

Colin There's not a leaf on it.
Mary It's been dead a long time.
Dickon Roses have climbed over it though. It won't look dead when they
    come into bloom. You wait, it'll be t' prettiest tree in t' garden.
Colin It looks as if a branch broke off at some time. I wonder how that
    happened.

Mary and Dickon exchange awkward glances

   The robin appears

Mary The robin! There he is, look! Over there!

Colin is diverted

Colin He's beautiful … He looks very busy.
Dickon He's foraging. Watch him close. If there's a worm anywhere he'll
    have it.

*Colin watches the robin. As he does so, Dickon and Mary exchange a quick
word*

Mary I think it must have been Magic sent the robin just then.
Dickon He mustn't find out how that branch broke. Not yet any road.

   The robin exits

Colin He's gone …
Dickon He'll be back.
Colin I never want this afternoon to end. I'll come here tomorrow and the
    day after, and the day after that. Now I've seen the spring, I want to see the
    summer. I want to watch everything coming alive.
Dickon Tha'll be running about same as us before long.
Colin Running?
Dickon Well, tha's got legs, han't tha?
Colin But they're so thin and weak.
Dickon There's no wonder, if tha' never uses 'em.
Colin But they always shake so. I'm afraid to stand on them.

Dickon Well, stop being afraid, tha'll stand fine then.

Ben Weatherstaff appears, peering over the wall

Colin Look — up there!
Ben I thought I heard some'at!
Mary Ben Weatherstaff! (*She moves over and stands beneath Ben*)

Ben doesn't at first notice Colin and Dickon

Ben So it's thee is it! You young bad 'un! If tha' were a wench o' mine, I'd
give thi a good hidin'! However in t' world did tha' manage to get in there?
Mary The robin showed me.
Ben Tha's even got cheek to lay t' badness on a robin, has tha?
Colin Wheel me over there, Dickon! Wheel me over!

Dickon wheels Colin over to the wall

You! You up there! Do you know who I am?

Ben struggles to speak. Nothing comes out

What's the matter with you? Answer me! Do you know who I am?
Ben Aye ... How could I not — wi' thi' mother's eyes staring out o' thi face
like some sort o' ghost? Tha'r her lad — one as is going to die.
Colin (*furiously*) Die? Who's told you I'm going to die? Who said that? How
dare you tell me I'm going to die? Dickon! Mary! Come here! Help me!
(*He tosses the cover off his legs*) Help me up! Help me out of this chair!

Dickon and Mary help Colin to stand

Now let go! Let go!

Dickon and Mary let go of Colin and he stands unaided

Look! Look at me, you! Look at me! Do I look as though I'm going to die?
Do I? Well do I?
Ben Well I'll be danged! Tha' can stand straighter than I can.
Colin There's nothing wrong with me — nothing at all — is there Dickon?
Dickon Nowt that time won't cure.
Ben Eeh, the stories folks invent! I were told tha'd never grow beyond a lad!
Colin Well, I will, see! I will grow! And this garden is going to make sure
of it! But that's a secret — so you're not to say anything. Do you

understand? You're not to breathe a word to anyone. Get down from that
ladder, I want to talk to you.
Ben Eh lad! I mean "Yes, sir." Yes, sir! At once, sir!
Mary I'll open the door for him.

Ben disappears

Mary exits

Colin Look at me, Dickon. Look at me. Is it you doing this? Is it like charming
animals? Are you making Magic?
Dickon Tha'r makin' all t' Magic thi'sen.
Colin I'm going to try and walk over to that tree.

Colin walks unsteadily across the stage. When he is half way across:

Mary and Ben Weatherstaff arrive

You see, Ben Weatherstaff. It's a lie, what everyone says. I'm not going
to die. I'm not!
Ben World's full o' fools all brayin' like jackasses. Tha's got too much pluck
in thi to die.

Colin takes another step and falls. Dickon and Mary run to help him up

Mary You need to practise, that's all. Like I did when I was learning to skip.
Ben Sit thi down, lad, and tell me what tha' wanted to say.

Colin sits in his chair

Colin What work do you do in the gardens?
Ben Owt I'm told.
Mary Ben knows all about gardens. He can do anything.
Ben Not any more. They only keep me on out o' favour – 'cos she liked me.
Colin She?
Ben Thi' mother.
Colin This was her garden, wasn't it.
Ben It were that. And she were right fond of it.
Colin Well it's my garden now, and I'm fond of it too. I'm going to come
here every day. Dickon and my cousin are making it come alive again.
Ben I can see that. By t' looks o'n it, they're makin' a good job an' all.
Colin Sometimes I might send for you to come and help.
Ben I'd be right glad to.

Colin But it must be a secret. You mustn't tell anyone. No-one must see you
    coming here.
Ben I've come here afore and no-one saw me.
Mary What? You've been in here? When?
Ben Last time were about two year back. I used to come in regular.
Mary But there was no door and no key.
Ben I never came through t' door. I come over t' wall.
Dickon So it was you did that prunin'. I might've guessed.
Ben Your mother loved these roses. They were like children to her. "Ben,"
    she says to me once, "if ever I go away you must promise to take care of
    them for me." So I did; once every year I'd come over t' wall — until t'
    rheumatics stopped me.
Colin You won't have to climb over the wall any more, you can come
    through the door — but only when I send for you to come and help Mary
    and Dickon.
Mary What about you?
Colin What do you mean?
Mary Well aren't you going to help as well?
Colin Me?
Mary There's an awful lot to do.
Colin Do you think I could?

Mary picks up a trowel and offers it to Colin. He hesitates

Mary You can do it.

*Colin takes the trowel. From a sitting position, he struggles to push it into the
earth. With his weak hands and wrists, he fails*

   You can do it, I tell you! You can do it!

Colin tries again

Dickon Push. Push it down. Deep into t' earth! Push!

Colin summons all his strength and finally succeeds

Colin I did it — I did it!
Ben Tha'r a Yorkshire lad for sure!
Colin This is just the first day and I almost walked and I've dug a hole —
    by myself!
Dickon Diggin' a hole's only t' first part. Tha mun plant some'at in it.
Colin I haven't got anything to plant.

Ben I can fetch thi a rose if tha' wants.
Colin Yes! Yes, I do want! Do it now, Weatherstaff! Go and get it! Quick!
What are you waiting for? Go on! Hurry up, will you! Go and get it!

Ben struggles off as fast as he can

(*To Mary*) Why are you looking at me like that?
Mary I'm thinking it must be getting your own way all the time that makes
you so rude.
Colin Was I rude?
Mary If you'd been one of the village lads Ben would never have allowed
you speak to him like that.
Colin He's a servant. That's how you speak to servants.
Mary I suppose I'm rude too ... I don't think I'm as rude as I was before I
started coming in the garden though.
Colin There's Magic in this garden, isn't there. Maybe not real Magic — but
we can pretend it is.
Mary It is real Magic! It is!

Ben returns with a rose

Ben Here, lad — set that in t' earth and it'll grow as strong as thee.

Colin plants the rose. As he does so:

*Music plays and the Lights change. The music swells and continues; as it does
so, the garden is added to. Roses and flowers begin to appear everywhere.
We move on in time — from spring into summer*

*The characters delight in the visible transformation taking place around
them*

The Music ends and the Lights change to evening shadows

Colin (*sitting*) I want you all to listen. I have an important announcement to
make.
Ben Ay ay, sir.

Colin prepares himself to make a speech

Colin I used to think I was never going to grow to be a man – but since I started
coming here, into the garden, all that's changed. I *am* going to grow up, I
know that for sure, and when I do — I'm going to be a scientist.

Ben Ay ay, sir.

Colin I shall make scientific discoveries — about Magic.

Ben Ay ay, sir.

Colin No-one knows very much about Magic you see — except Mary, because she was born in India, and Dickon, because he can charm animals.

Mary And boys.

Colin I'd never seen things grow before. Not like this — pushing out of the earth, getting stronger every day. "What's doing it?" I kept wondering. "What's making it happen?" Well, I don't know what it is — but I'm going to call it Magic.

Ben Ay ay sir.

Colin There's no need to keep saying that, Weatherstaff.

Ben Ay ay s … (*He stops himself*)

Colin If Magic can make plants and flowers grow strong, perhaps it can make me strong too — as strong as Dickon. That's my first experiment … The trouble is I don't know how to start.

Mary There are people in India who say words over and over again, thousands of times, until it stays in their minds forever. I think it's like that with Magic. If you keep calling for it, in the end it comes.

Colin Is that true, Dickon?

Dickon It's only t' same as birds callin' out for t' dawn.

Colin What do we have to do?

Mary You have to be still — very still and very quiet.

Pause

Colin What now?

Mary Imagine we're in some sort of temple.

Colin Do you think we should sway backwards and forwards?

Ben I'm not doin' no swayin', not wi' my rheumatics!

Colin The Magic will take your rheumatics away!

Ben I'm still not doin' no swayin'.

Mary We'll not do any swaying — we'll just chant.

Ben I'm not doin' no chantin' neither. Last time I tried chantin' I got chucked out o t' church choir!

Colin I'll chant. I'll chant on my own. (*He prepares himself*)

The others wait in anticipation

What shall I chant?

Mary It doesn't matter. Whatever comes into your head. The Magic will come.

There is silence again

Colin (*chanting*) The sun is shining.
                That is Magic.
                The flowers are growing.
                That is Magic.
                Being alive
                That is Magic.
                Magic! Magic!
                Come and help me!   *Animals start to appear*
                Make me strong!
                Magic! Magic!   **Mary** It's working! Look, the
                Come and help me!   creatures! The creatures are
                Make me strong!   coming!
                Magic! Magic!
                Come and help me!   *Ben starts to nod off*
                Make me strong!
                Magic! Magic!
                Come and help me!
                Make me strong!

Colin stops and waits in silence for the magic to arrive

Ben starts to snore. Dickon gives him a dig

Dickon (*whispering*) Ben …
Ben What's up?
Dickon Tha's dozed off!
Ben (*pulling himself together*) Nowt o' t' sort!

Music plays, quietly at first and building during the following

*Unaided, Colin slowly draws himself to his feet and starts to walk, slightly
unsteadily at first. The creatures accompany him*

Colin   The Magic is in me.
                The Magic is in me.
                The Magic is in me.
Mary You can do it — you can do it.

The music continues to build

*Colin's walk becomes more confident and rhythmic, gradually developing
into a dance, growing all the time*

Colin   The Magic is in me!
                   The Magic is in me!
                   The Magic is in me!

Colin whirls and dances around the garden. The others join in too. The dance moves into a more stylized form, taking on an Indian influence and building to a climax. Eventually it stops

   The creatures exit

The music fades out

Colin It worked. The experiment worked. The Magic came.

Ben I've never seen owt like that in my life.

Mary What's Mrs Medlock going to say when she finds out?

Colin She isn't going to find out. She won't be told. No-one is to know anything — not until I'm nearly as strong as Dickon. Then my father — he'll be the first to know.

Mary He won't be able to believe his eyes! He'll think he's in a dream.

Colin When he comes home, when he sees how strong the garden's made me, perhaps he won't hate me any more.

Ben God bless thi, lad — we'll have thi as strong as a prizefighter! Before tha's done tha'll be like a champion wrestler!

Colin Weatherstaff. That is disrespectful; I shall not be like a wrestler.

Ben Beg pardon, sir. Beg pardon.

Dickon Hold on, maybe Ben's right ... Does tha' know Bob Howarth from Thwaite?

Ben Know him? He's strongest chap on t' moor is Bob Howarth!

Dickon A champion wrestler! I asked him once if he did 'owt extra to make himself so strong.

Colin What did he say?

Dickon He said he did.

Mary What? What does he do?

Dickon He eats a lot. Eggs, bread, milk, 'taters. As much as he can get down.

Mary Colin can't do that. If he starts eating a lot, Mrs Medlock will suspect straight away. She's always complaining about his lack of appetite.

Ben That's true. She's said as much to me.

Dickon But he'll never get strong if he dun't eat.

Colin Then I'll eat in secret! ... Out here! In the garden!

Dickon Eat what?

Colin Weatherstaff, you're to go to the village and bring eggs and potatoes and milk and anything else Dickon tells you to buy! You're to do it every day and you mustn't breathe a word to anyone — especially Mrs Medlock!

(*He hands Ben some money*) Here's some money. I'll give you more
tomorrow.

Ben Ay ay, sir!

Colin (*as the rajah*) You have my permission to go.

Ben exits chuckling

Mary I'll eat here as well! We won't need any meals at the Manor at all then!
I wonder what Mrs Medlock will make of that!

They all laugh

Dickon There's some'at else tha' mun do — exercises. Bob Howarth does
'em every day; he showed me – arms, legs, every muscle in t' body.

Colin How does he do them? Show me, Dickon! Show me!

Dickon Tha' has to do 'em gentle at first. Tha dun't want to strain thi'sen.

Colin I'll be careful, I promise. Oh, Dickon. You're the most Magic boy in
the world!

Dickon Watch.

Music plays very softly

*Dickon demonstrates exercises and Mary and Colin copy them, softly
chanting out the exercises. Once this is established:*

*The Lights cross-fade to a separate area of the stage, somewhere in the
Manor*

*The exercises continue, the chanting and music softly underscoring the
following dialogue*

*Mrs Medlock and Martha enter the lit area of the stage. Martha carries a
tray with two unfinished meals on it*

Martha I'm afraid there's no improvement, ma'am. I don't know what
we're going to do.

Mrs Medlock (*examining the tray*) They're a pair o' young Satans, that they
are! Not a mouthful of that lovely young fowl. And that bread sauce hasn't
had a fork in it!

Martha Whenever I try to say owt they just burst out laughing. I don't know
what's up with 'em.

Mrs Medlock They'll starve themselves into their graves if they carry on like
this. They've reduced that poor woman in the kitchen to tears. She *invented*
a pudding for them yesterday, and back it went, not even touched.

Martha The funny part is, ma'am, you'd swear Master Colin was putting on weight. His face is fillin' out like a ripe tomato and his skin's losing that horrible waxy colour it al'us had.

Mrs Medlock The girl's the same. She was as plain as a plucked crow when she first came — you'd almost think she was pretty now … You don't think she's casting some sort of magic spell, do you?

Martha Magic spell, ma'am?

Mrs Medlock I wouldn't put it past her. I wouldn't put anything past that one! Thank goodness Mr Craven's well out of the way, that's all I can say. Goodness knows what he'd have to say if he knew any of this!

Martha and Mrs Medlock both exit

The Lights cross-fade back to the children in the garden still chanting their exercises

The children continue for a few moments and stop

The music fades out

Colin My arms and legs feel so full of Magic I can hardly keep them still. It's working, isn't it? The food. The exercises. It's all working.

Dickon Martha can't understand it. She says Mrs Medlock thinks it's Mary working magic.

Mary It's the garden that's working the magic. It's worked on both of us.

Colin I wish Father would come. I want to show him. I'm ready now. I want him to see me … Why doesn't he come? Where is he?

Dickon He's bound to come home soon.

Colin But what will he say? What if he's not pleased? What if he still hates me?

Dickon He doesn't hate you.

Colin He does! I know he does! You don't know him! Not like I do! He's always hated me – ever since I was born!

Pause. A moment's gloom

The robin enters

Mary Look. The robin. He's come to see what's going on.

Dickon He can't weigh up all this pushin' and stretchin' and bendin' … Tha' dun't know about Bob Haworth's exercises, does tha', little 'un.

Mary He knows about Magic, though. He knows every secret in this garden.

Music plays and the Lights dim

The children remain where they are during the following

The robin takes flight. We follow him in a pin-spot of light on a journey around the stage. As the journey comes to an end:

> *The Lights comes up on Mr Craven in a separate area. He is sitting, alone and thoughtful*

The robin alights nearby, singing. Mr Craven looks up

The music continues softly during the following

Mr Craven What are you singing about, little robin? Something happy? You've picked the wrong man for a song like that.

The robin hops nearer, still singing

> Don't you understand? I came here to try and forget things like you.

The robin moves very close to Mr Craven

> There was a time … The song of a bird. The curve of a petal. The smell of roses … A garden.

Colin The Magic is in me.
Mr Craven (*jumping up, startled*) Colin?
Colin The Magic is in me!
Mr Craven (*looking around for the source of the voice*) Colin — Colin — Where are you?
Colin The Magic is in me!
Mr Craven Is this some sort of dream?

The robin flutters around Mr Craven, singing

> The garden — the garden!

> *Mr Craven hurries off*

The music swells. The robin flies back to the children in its pin-spot of light. The music ends

The Lights come up on a separate stage area

Mr Craven enters followed by a flustered Mrs Medlock

Mrs Medlock I'm afraid nothing's ready, sir. If we'd known you were coming … We weren't expecting you home till the autumn … I'll get Martha to make up the ——

Mr Craven Leave it, Medlock. Leave it. It will do later. The boy. Tell me how the boy is!

Mrs Medlock The boy, sir?

Mr Craven Colin. My son, Colin. How's Colin?

Mrs Medlock Well he's — he's ——

Mr Craven He's not … Don't tell me he's … He's not worse is he?

Mrs Medlock Not exactly, sir. Not in a manner speaking.

Mr Craven What then? Tell me! How is he?

Mrs Medlock He's … He's … He's different.

Mr Craven Different? How is he different? What do you mean?

Mrs Medlock None of us can rightly make out, sir. His appetite is beyond mortal understanding.

Mr Craven Has he become more — more peculiar?

Mrs Medlock That's it, sir! That's it! Peculiar, he's become very peculiar.

Mr Craven Oh my God … How does he look?

Mrs Medlock It's his eating, sir … To look at him you'd say he was putting on flesh, but we're afraid it may be some sort of bloat … He's started laughing too.

Mr Craven Laughing?

Mrs Medlock Martha's heard him! With that young vixen from India. Nothing in this house has been right since she arrived.

Mr Craven I must see him. Where is he?

Mrs Medlock We tried to stop him, sir. We did everything we could. There was just no reasoning with him. I blame that ——

Mr Craven Medlock. Just tell me where he is!

Mrs Medlock In the garden, sir. He won't allow a human creature near him!

Mr Craven The garden! Of course! Don't you see, Medlock? It wasn't a dream at all! It was magic! Some form of magic!

Mr Craven dashes off

Mrs Medlock watches in bewilderment

Mrs Medlock Magic … So it's true? She *has* bewitched him. She's bewitched us all!

Mrs Medlock exits in a flap

The Lights cross-fade to the children

> *The children play a game of tig in the garden, laughing and running and shouting*

> *Mr Craven enters the garden. He slowly approaches the children and gazes in astonishment at them for a few moments before they see him*

Colin sees Mr Craven and stops in his tracks. They stare at each other in silence

Mr Craven Colin?
Colin Father …

There is a pause. Mr Craven can't believe his eyes

> I've been waiting for you … I didn't want anyone else to know … It was the garden … The Magic.
Mr Craven Magic?
Colin Mary and Dickon. It's been our secret. I wanted you to be the first.
Mr Craven Me?
Colin I thought when you saw me, maybe ——
Mr Craven Maybe what?
Colin — maybe you wouldn't hate me any more.
Mr Craven You think I hated you?
Colin I've been doing Bob Howarth's exercises. I do them every day. I can beat Mary at running, can't I, Mary?
Mr Craven What have I done? Oh, my sweet child. All these years. What have I done?
Colin You're not angry then?
Mr Craven Angry? I'm the happiest father in the world.

Mr Craven takes hold of Colin and clutches him tight. There is a long powerful moment of reunion

Mary It was the garden. We'll show you if you like.

They all move to set off round the garden

> *Mrs Medlock bustles in with Martha. Mrs Medlock does not see Colin, who is hidden behind the others*

Mrs Medlock Merciful heavens! I swear on my life, sir, I never knew they'd come here! Never! *She*'s the one behind this! That little heathen and her magic spells! No wonder no-one's ever been able to find you all these months! I knew she was trouble, the moment she stepped off that boat! Where's Master Colin? Come on! Tell Mr Craven what you've done with him! If you've worked any of your sorcery on him I'll ——

Colin (*stepping into view*) Stop fussing will you, Medlock! You're always fussing!

Mrs Medlock Master Colin? Master Colin. (*She falls into a dead faint*)

They all laugh

Music creeps in

Mr Craven I thought it would all be dead.

Mary I thought that too. It came alive again.

Colin It's been our secret.

Mr Craven There've been too many secrets. We've locked away so many bad thoughts there was no room for any good ones. It wasn't you I hated, Colin. It was the whole world. Not any more. From now on this garden will always be open. Open and breathing and alive.

Mary As wick as thee and me, eh Colin?

They all laugh

The music swells. They help up Mrs Medlock

Mr Craven leads them all into a dance of celebration and life

The Lights fade

The final image is Mary very much part of a family

CURTAIN

FURNITURE AND PROPERTY LIST

ACT I

Tripod, camera and flashpan (**Photographer**)
Suitcases (**Father**)
Dresses (**Mother**)
Wooden pipe (**Dickon**)
Penknife (**Dickon**)
Mary's bedroom furniture — chair and small table
Tray with food and crockery (**Martha**)
Scarf for **Martha**
Book (**Mary**)
Skipping rope (**Martha**)
Key for **Mary**
Bell for **Mr Craven**
Candle for **Mary**
Painting (**Stage Management**)
Statue (**Stage Management**)
Tapestry (**Stage Management**)
Bath chair and cover for **Colin**
Cord
Portrait of young woman

ACT II

Feeding-bottle (**Dickon**)
Bright flowers and greenery
Feather
Trowel
More flowers and roses
Tray with two unfinished meals on it (**Martha**)

LIGHTING PLOT

To open: Darkness

| Cue 1 | Music; when ready | (Page 1) |
| | *Bring up lights on* **Mary** | |

| Cue 2 | **Mary** falls asleep; sounds fade | (Page 3) |
| | *Dim lights* | |

| Cue 3 | Ship's siren; music swells | (Page 3) |
| | *Change lights to ship setting* | |

| Cue 4 | The ship actors exit | (Page 4) |
| | *Fade lights to spot on* **Mary** | |

ACT I

| Cue 5 | Set changes to **Mary**'s room | (Page 4) |
| | *Bring up lights on* **Mary**'*s room* | |

| Cue 6 | **Martha** exits | (Page 7) |
| | *Change lights to non-naturalistic setting* | |

| Cue 7 | **Mary** comes to a stop. Music ends | (Page 8) |
| | *Change lights to outdoor setting* | |

| Cue 8 | **Ben** exits. Music | (Page 9) |
| | *Change lights to* **Mary**'*s room setting; late evening effect* | |

| Cue 9 | **Martha** exits | (Page 13) |
| | *Change lights for set change* | |

| Cue 10 | **Ben** and **Mary** arrive in the garden. Music fades out | (Page 13) |
| | *Change lights to outdoor setting* | |

| Cue 11 | **Mary** pushes the door. Music | (Page 14/15) |
| | *Change lights to magical state* | |

| Cue 12 | **Mary** passes into the garden | (Page 15) |
| | *Return lights to outdoor state* | |

Cue 13   The ivy wall is moved back   (Page 15)
              Cross-fade lights to wall exterior

Cue 14   **Mary** leads **Dickon** though the wall. Music   (Page 16)
              Change lights to secret garden setting

Cue 15   **Dickon**: " ... as safe as that robin's." Music   (Page 18)
              Change lights to interior setting

Cue 16   **Mary**: "I can have my garden!" Music   (Page 20)
              Change lights to night-time shadows

Cue 17   **Mary** lights a candle   (Page 21)
              Bring up covering spot on candle

Cue 18   **Mary** pushes the door open. Music ends   (Page 21)
              *Bring up dim light on **Colin**'s room*

Cue 19   **Mary** strokes **Colin**'s hand   (Page 24)
              Fade all lights to black-out

ACT II

To open: Darkness

Cue 20   Music   (Page 25)
              Bring up lights on secret garden setting

Cue 21   **Mary**: " ... this very day!" Music   (Page 26)
              Change lighting to hall setting

Cue 22   **Mary** exits. Music   (Page 29)
              *Change lighting to **Colin**'s room setting*

Cue 23   **Colin**: "I shall see it!" Music   (Page 32)
              "Stylized journey" lighting ending with garden setting

Cue 24   **Colin** plants the rose. Music   (Page 37)
              Change lights from spring to summer setting

Cue 25   Music ends   (Page 37)
              Fade lights to evening shadows

Cue 26   **Dickon**, **Colin** and **Mary** do exercises   (Page 41)
              Cross-fade lights to separate area of stage; interior

Cue 27   **Martha** and **Mrs Medlock** exit   (Page 42)
              Cross-fade lights back to children

Cue 28   **Mary**: " ... every secret in this garden." Music   (Page 42)
          Dim lights

Cue 29   The robin takes flight   (Page 43)
          Pin-spot follows robin

Cue 30   Robin arrives by **Mr Craven**   (Page 43)
          Bring up lights on **Mr Craven**

Cue 31   **Mr Craven** hurries off. Music swells   (Page 43)
          Pin-spot follows robin

Cue 32   Music ends   (Page 43)
          Cut pin spot on robin; bring up lights on separate stage area

Cue 33   **Mrs Medlock** exits   (Page 44)
          Cross-fade lights to children

Cue 34   Dance   (Page 46)
          Fade lights

EFFECTS PLOT

Cue 13   **Mary** reaches the ivy-covered door   (Page 8)
             Fade music

Cue 14   **Ben** exits   (Page 9)
             Music

Cue 15   **Martha** enters   (Page 10)
             Fade music; bring up distant recorded wailing

Cue 16   **Martha** exits; lights change   (Page 13)
             Music

Cue 17   **Mary** and **Ben** arrive in the garden   (Page 13)
             Fade music

Cue 18   **Mary** pushes the door open   (Page 14)
             Music

Cue 19   **Mary** stands for a moment, just gazing   (Page 15)
             Fade music

Cue 20   **Mary**: " ... so they can breathe!"   (Page 15)
             Music

Cue 21   Lights cross-fade to the exterior of the wall   (Page 15)
             Fade music

Cue 22   **Mary** leads **Dickon** through the ivy wall   (Page 16)
             Music

Cue 23   **Dickon** and **Mary** stand in the secret garden (Page 16)
             Fade music

Cue 24   **Dickon**: " ... as safe as that robin's."   (Page 18)
             Music

Cue 25   **Mary** runs to Mrs Medlock   (Page 18)
             Fade music

Cue 26   **Mary**: "I can have my garden."   (Page 20)
             Music

Cue 27   **Martha**: "Look at the rain."   (Page 20)
             Distant recorded wailing

Cue 28   **Martha**: " ... one o' these days."   (Page 20)
             Distant recorded wailing

Cue 29	**Mary** steps through the door *Fade music*	(Page 21)
Cue 30	**Mary**: "Shut your eyes." *Music*	(Page 24)

ACT II

Cue 31	When ready *Music*	(Page 25)
Cue 32	Establish **Mary** and **Dickon** working in the garden *Fade music*	(Page 25)
Cue 33	**Mary**: " ... this very day!" *Music*	(Page 26)
Cue 34	**Mary** enters *Fade music*	(Page 26)
Cue 35	**Mary** exits *Music*	(Page 29)
Cue 36	**Colin**'s room is set up *Fade music*	(Page 29)
Cue 37	**Colin**: "I shall really see it!" *Music*	(Page 32)
Cue 38	**Colin** covers his eyes *Music swells*	(Page 32)
Cue 39	Establish greener garden *Fade music*	(Page 32)
Cue 40	**Colin** plants the rose *Music*	(Page 37)
Cue 41	The lights change *Swell music*	(Page 37)
Cue 42	Establish characters enjoying the transformation *Fade music*	(Page 37)
Cue 43	**Ben**: "Nowt o' t' sort!" *Music, quiet then building*	(Page 39)

11/04 .

Cue 44 Creatures exit (Page 40)
Fade music

Cue 45 **Dickon**: "Watch." (Page 41)
Music; very soft

Cue 46 Children stop exercising (Page 42)
Fade music

Cue 47 **Mary**: " ... secret in this garden." (Page 42)
Music

Cue 48 **Mr Craven** hurries off (Page 43)
Swell music

Cue 49 Robin flies back to the children (Page 43)
Fade music

Cue 50 They all laugh (Page 46)
Music

Cue 51 They all laugh (Page 46)
Swell music